Waspfish

Val Dering Rojas

Glass Lyre Press

Copyright © 2016 Val Dering Rojas

Paperback ISBN: 978-1-941783-22-1

All rights reserved: except for the purpose of quoting brief passages for review, no part of this book may be reproduced or transmitted in any form or by any means, electronic or mechanical, including photocopying, recording, or by any information storage and retrieval system, without permission in writing from the publisher.

Cover art & Author photo: Samantha Rojas
Design & layout: Steven Asmussen
Copyediting: Linda E. Kim

Glass Lyre Press, LLC
P.O. Box 2693
Glenview, IL 60026
www.GlassLyrePress.com

Contents

Bird's Eye	11
I Dreamt Fire and Water	12
Let's Consider Her the Waspfish	14
With Miniature House	15
Phone Call from the Pleasure Center	16
Conchology	17
Mania	18
A Brief Guide to Bird as Dervish	19
How to Catch a Fish with Your Bare Hands	20
Saint Dymphna by the Sea	21
In the Body Garden	22
Postcard from Space	23
In the Monastery of the Angels	24
How to Leave the World	25
Rhinochimaera, Filmed and Preserved	26
Loss	27
The Nostalgia of Losing a Map	28
Angling	29
Notes	31
Acknowledgments	32
About the Author	33

For the ones I love.

The animals you drove away are back
to walk the streets with eyes like glittering wounds

    —Malinda Markham, "Menagerie"

Bird's Eye

And anyway, doesn't every one of us live right where we are?

Center of gravity in our chests, lungs pushed up against our spines?

Keel of breastbone, camber of wing, a feather, a digit, a thumb, fulcrum;

a river of rattlesnake, a conglomeration of lagoon, tangle of beetles

on a freeway of skin. Destiny entangled with destination.

But you know it's something much closer than that.

A map pin or it's pin dot,

or the scent of the smoke from the burning bones

and lampblack

used to make the ink

that first drew the map.

I Dreamt Fire and Water

was within your body, was,

I tell you,

still burned into me,

and the arc which occurs

when one strikes the other.

There are things—

(the sting of whiskey)

that I should have,

(and the rushing of

fire on fire)

I should say, resisted,

for the reasons teaspoons

know the taste of oxidation.

There is no science

which knows my fear

of how the land will love us,

lost in soft green moss,

how it trusts we know

what to burn, what to feed,

because there are places

(the encroaching lake)

that will not differentiate,

(my tempered passion)

cool from cold,

sublimation from apathy.

Let's Consider Her the Waspfish

with her hungry weight of wings like waves

and the way she spills salt like venom. Let's say her heart

lugs ships full of the dead, and that this deadwood

has been chewed into nests, breasts plump

with seawater. Let's say our questions are her unctuous cures:

how the fleshy insides of a fig can be denied; what it is

to devour the sweet, viscid larvae of the bee; why a stung girl

refuses to weep. Let's consider her with the tide, how she

comes and goes, or the way a compass-rose

wheels within her chest.

Let's say blessed are those whose bodies become offerings in the surf.

Let's gawk at these awkward fruits washed upon the sand.

Let's will them from rot to sugar.

With Miniature House

Not because she wanted to abandon this domesticity
or even because she crafted snapped twigs

into tiny fuses. Not because she had been hiding them
under her mattress for months: these minute peelings

of bark and sorrow. Or how many days smoke
could be seen through the keyhole.

First she was paper, once wood. Wood, once tree.
The tree, hewn box which holds her. She might have

been anything. Like tinder, fuel, kindling. Or one
timbered beam— sudden sky, heavenly opening.

She was that, or she was the taciturn timbrel of unfolding.
It could have been the curtains crafted from cut snow:

lace paper flakes the color of curdled cream. In the kitchen,
a table strewn with stationery, pen. It could have been

that she's written an argument for longevity, tissue-thin:
perfume your head. Bake diminutive cakes. Wear your

death-dress, while breathing.

Phone Call from the Pleasure Center

Cup your ear with my hand, Dear, I know the held air
pushed up against your lungs—remember when
I was enough to gratify your young and sun-browned
life? I am your steamed crab feasts, fresh lake trout,
spoon bread. The drunken rush of beer, of eating more
almonds than anyone could count. What did you leave
behind the boathouse besides the miracle of escape or
the conspiracy of warm blood? How is it that your pockets
are full with saltwater taffy swiped from the boardwalk, yet
the sting of sugar from each pink center always tastes
of emptiness? Are there still recollections of how to lie
in the shallow surf and feel in your ear, the tickle of salt
and sand? How is it now, to keep your body corpsestill?
To lie alone in the excruciating dark?

Conchology

The shells in the chiffonier are glass islands. You closeted them
using a sailor's system of making knots; opted
for a cupboard as a way to shield your freckles from the sun; forgot
the sound of unlatching. Each island: classification, diagnosis:
(tiny) *butterfly* , (tiny) *open heart* , (tiny) *skeleton* . Blame the temblor
for why the waves come in code: smallsmalllargesmalltsunami.
The door opened, and an entire ecosystem surfaced: bivalves,
gastropods, cephalopods, polyplacophora, tube sponge, algae bloom.
And the carapace of an urchin, which is called a *test*.
But this is not tribulation. This is not the sea leaving your veins.
This is not a crucible of salt. This is the whelk prying open
the oyster's shell. This is the crab taking the whelk. This is
the albatross swallowing the crab. This is everything,
feeding off of everything else.

Mania

Tell me how
    I am thorn, pincer,
        barb, crook.
The cassowary with the ruinous disposition,
      the footed blade.

        Or the hawk moth and its nightly flirt,
            its scorch of moon,
                its cacophony of sting.

Tell me how
    I am cougar,
        jaguar, cheetah.
How I am the rattler in the brush
    ready to strike.   Tell me how
            I become propellant and accelerant
                and spark and torch
How the scrub of me is dry
      and tinder-ripe.
    Tell me that you can see the iridescence
        of gasoline on my lips,
           this struck match
                between   my teeth.

A Brief Guide to Bird as Dervish

When you say that I am okay, I hear *birdsong*,
brain-din of hummingbird wing, chant of herring-gull heart,
a belly filled with rubble. When you speak, your voice is tundra,
is treeless and achingly low, and I think mourning dove, rock dove,
and how many larks must it take to make an exaltation.

First, it was the jay's hoarded seed, the story caught
in her protracted throat. It was the beechnut buried in the yard,
the missing tombstone of twigs. Then, the jay herself, greedily
collecting but keeping none; poverty regrowing forests of oak, new trees
springing from acorns never-unearthed and unclaimed.

Now, my woozy sky, my whirling Earth. For rebirth to be pulled
from my breast, and this cloak of feathers to be plucked from my back,
for affliction to become starling, star: say that I am okay so I can speak
charm, ascension, wisdom. And say it again, because at this speed,
birdsong sounds like turbine.

How to Catch a Fish with Your Bare Hands

Be a branch, cooling palm, root
of fingers. Be a tree. Be the space
between rock and riverbank, the
come-hither nightwalker, lure
for hungry swimmers. Behold
her silver, behold her sinuousness,
her sinlessness, how she's glitter
magnified, a trinket for a magpie.
Behold the moon which lives
in her belly, and the jellied eyespots
black as swill. Aim for the gills. Make
a heart of index and thumb, find
the sweetness between cartilage
and bone. Amaze at the way the river
warps scales into pearls. Amaze
at the equilibrium of hands. At the way
her spine, brittle as clamshell,
is effortlessly riven.

Saint Dymphna by the Sea

When your flesh became a flaming, red-shelled lobster, and
your cavity blackened to aubergine

When your cheeks flushed at the face of your mother, your
head a cooling opal in your father's palms

You, with sword and book and lamp, and lilies in hand,
beat our hearts like chimes

And lay severed in the clover with us,
our faces strung together like rosaries.

In the Body Garden

You know how a body confesses. How it sings. How pilus and root
gather at the nape like nettled ropes; a dirty halo; a slipped crown.

Here, disclosed and disguised, you're the honeybee and blowfly.
You're blackout, you're balefire. You're meadowlark and crow.

You're the larder beetle. You're absurdity and the allure of suffering.
You're grace and what devours it.

Once, you craved the coolness of dark earth. Scattered teeth
like seeds. Let fingernails become twisted vines.

Once, you slept in the outline of black ants; sustenance
of nectar and flesh.

You spoke empty your secrets, made your mouth
a graceful blue blossom.

Now, you're tongue of knives and ear of opulent wound.
You know the quiet clatter a body can make—

that anyone who listens hard enough will hear its crime.

Postcard from Space

Dark here, and I'm writing you with the light of the moon, this disc of spine, this body of sky. The moon is an eye that is watching me like God, with its flecked iris, its face that never changes. Each night the moon's been a constricted pupil as I wait for it to explain loss and gain, and each night I'm reminded that the brightest thing out here is dark as coal. Last night, I thought of you turning towards our window, asking questions of falling stars, and my body broke into a thousand negative dots of sooty Rorschach. I try and clarify the importance of night glow and why I should avoid this lunatic moon, but by the time this reaches you and puddles in the hollows of your face, in the rut of your chin, you will already understand that I too am always slowing, forever angling away from your Earth.

In the Monastery of the Angels

This body will always reek of burnt wood, allspice, clove.

Inside, a moon like licorice. Black as tea. Bright as

a sugared cinnamon tongue: *I can persuade myself*

into anything.

And the way I measure distress: by depth of this obsession.

Crows that fly east to west; how long

they can remember a face; how long I'll continue

un-scavenged, unchanged.

And star anise, swarthy-skinned sky. Singe cleverly hidden.

The way I sweep small bones from this bed. A tiny pyre. And now,

these sweetmeats on my pillow; the low smoke of incense

like a suggestion.

I'll always be tar-dark wings, smoldering opaque as carbon.

The way breath beats from a lung. Lithe as flight. And for ballast,

an opium-heavy tongue: *I can't pray my way*

out of anything.

How to Leave the World

Not with lips dry, no praise for the wind. Not with Santa Anas
swishing through the trees, but with memories of ocean.

Not with a throat coated with the never-said, but
with a sky not quite seafoam.

Listen for the history of small things:
the grey-green noise a church bell makes, moths

tapping the ceiling; every full or empty bottle smashed,
a whisper of the neighbor's lovemaking.

Maybe you were right in thinking all creatures
eventually return to the aquatic, all things tidal. That it is

the voice of God, sonorous and delicate within the carapace
of a crab. Leave when you know the world to be

graceful and kind. Not today, when all is sweltering.

Rhinochimaera, Filmed and Preserved

This jar of water and salt. This

formaldehyde face. This is how

to explain ache. Alive, you are

elephantbutterfly,

deepest sea.

Darkness, sublimity. And I think, *Yes,*

this is how affliction looks

once it leaves the body.

Loss

    It begins and ends with disappearing.
That first effervescent super-ocean and Pangaea's
rifts and collisions. Ever one body losing its shape
to make another.

    And what leaves with loss? Say it slowly
and I don't recognize what's absent; the Great Pyramid
with its perfectly creased edge, grain by grain
secretly returning to sand.

    For proof, these small antiquities: worry stones
for mountains, empty shells for something once teeming.
And this abandoned cornucopia. A cup
running over with dust.

    And people are like this: they fall away as if scales from fish,
the way heat shimmers and swells—become the kind of water
that flashes like perception: brilliant for a moment,
then gone.

The Nostalgia of Losing a Map

Did you know that you are a falling bridge?
A collapsing star?

You are a nautical museum with less history
each day, secretly relocating the past
box by box.

I smell antiquity in the air, hear the corners
of dry pages crack off in the breeze.
I can taste the salt of worlds folding in.

Remember the darkness at Lakeside?
How every lit home became a beacon
for navigating the canal? Not everybody
is a falling bridge. Not everyone,
a collapsing star.

Everybody's darkness is different. Mercury
doesn't have to be in retrograde to light one of your
hundreds of Yankee Candles and pray for me.

Code Grey is is a great safeword if nobody
utters it.

We just let the unfocused landscape of distance
say what it wanted to say instead: days nesting
under thick shrubs, coming out to forage at night.
making yourself a ball of spines as defense.

Me, turning from vixen to solitary scream. Even
the ocean reversed its tide for a time.

Soon, the moon will be eclipsed and all will stop
for a moment. Come with me, I want you to
explode with biography, I want you to show me
all your lighthouses, all your shipwrecks.

Angling

A man catches a fish, and marvels at her luminosity. Porcelain skinned

specimen. He thinks of bones falling into fire, of feldspar, sodium,

seawater's silver-white equivalent, ground glass prism. He thinks

of the ashes of saints. He thinks of table salt and the translucence

of kaolin. How even the faintest light will expose flaws, cracks.

He thinks, how, when a man catches a fish, that sometimes,

he throws her back.

Notes

In "Phone Call from the Pleasure Center", the pleasure center refers to the *medial forebrain bundle*, also known as The Reward Center of the brain.

In "Saint Dymphna by the Sea" Saint Dymphna refers to the patron saint of the mentally ill, born in Ireland in the seventh century, daughter to a pagan Irish king and his Christian wife. When Dymphna was 14, her mother died, and her father, so deeply in love with his wife fell into mental illness and loneliness. When it was suggested he remarry, he began to desire his daughter because she so resembled her deceased mother. When Dymphna learned of this, she fled to Belgium, where her father eventually found her. She resisted his wishes to return to Ireland and marry, so enraging her father that he beheaded her.

"In The Monastery of the Angels" was inspired by the monastery of cloistered nuns of the Dominican Order in Los Angeles, California, of the same name.

"Rhinochimaera, Filmed and Preserved" was inspired by the short film by NOAA Ship Okeanos Explorer, Northeast U.S. Canyons 2013 Expedition, "Rhinochimera", July 13, 2013, available on YouTube.

"The Nostalgia of Losing a Map" is for E.A.D.

Acknowledgments

Thanks to the editors and staff of the following publications where these poems first appeared, often in earlier forms.

> BURNTDISTRICT: A Brief Guide to Bird as Dervish
> CRACK THE SPINE: With Miniature House
> CSHS QUARTERLY JOURNAL: In the Body Garden, In the Monastery of the Angels, Loss
> PIRENE'S FOUNTAIN: Conchology
> RIGHT HAND POINTING: Angling, Rhinochimaera: Filmed and Preserved
> TEN CHAPBOOK, DANCING GIRL PRESS, 2014; FLUTTER POETRY JOURNAL 2013: Postcard from Space

With deepest gratitude to Jessie Carty, Corey Mesler, Donna Vorreyer, Michael C. Kitchen, Ami Kaye and the entire Glass Lyre Press family.

About the Author

Val Dering Rojas is a Los Angeles based poet and artist who has also studied Addiction and Recovery Counseling and Psychology. She is the author of the chapbook *TEN* (Dancing Girl Press, 2014) and a Pushcart nominee. Val believes water is what keeps her in coastal Los Angeles, as she is attracted to water of many kinds: bathwater, pool water, ocean water and tears. When not writing, Val enjoys busking poems at the beaches of Venice, CA.

Glass Lyre Press

exceptional works to replenish the spirit

Glass Lyre Press is an independent literary publisher interested in technically accomplished, stylistically distinct, and original work. Glass Lyre seeks diverse writers that possess a dynamic aesthetic and an ability to emotionally and intellectually engage a wide audience of readers.

Glass Lyre's vision is to connect the world through language and art. We hope to expand the scope of poetry and short fiction for the general reader through exceptionally well-written books, which evoke emotion, provide insight, and resonate with the human spirit.

Poetry Collections
Poetry Chapbooks
Select Short & Flash Fiction
Anthologies

www.GlassLyrePress.com

www.ingramcontent.com/pod-product-compliance
Lightning Source LLC
Chambersburg PA
CBHW021200080526
44588CB00008B/436